THE OTHER LOVER

PHOENIX **POETS**

A SERIES EDITED BY ALAN SHAPIRO

The *Other* Lover

BRUCE SMITH

THE UNIVERSITY OF CHICAGO PRESS
Chicago and London

Bruce Smith teaches in the writing program at the University of Alabama. His previous collections of poetry are *The Common Wages*, *Silver and Information* (National Poetry Series Selection), and *Mercy Seat* (University of Chicago Press).

The University of Chicago Press, Chicago 60637
The University of Chicago Press, Ltd., London
© 2000 by The University of Chicago
All rights reserved. Published 2000

09 08 07 06 05 04 03 02 01 00   2 3 4 5

ISBN 0-226-76407-9 (cloth)
      0-226-76408-7 (paper)

Library of Congress Cataloging-in-Publication Data

Smith, Bruce, 1946–
      The other lover / Bruce Smith.
            p.   cm.   -- (Phoenix poets)
      ISBN 0-226-76407-9 (alk. paper). -- ISBN 0-226-76408-7 (pbk. : alk. paper)
      I. Title.   II. Series.
PS3569.M512084   2000
811' . 54--dc21   99-22588
                                                                         CIP

For Chard deNiord

#439

Undue Significance a starving man attaches
to Food—
Far off—He sighs—and therefore—Hopeless—
And therefore—Good—

Partaken—it relieves—indeed—
But proves us
That Spices fly
In the Receipt—It was the Distance—
Was Savory—

Emily Dickinson

"Every work of art is an uncommitted crime."

Theodor Adorno

Contents

Acknowledgments

The author wishes to thank the editors of the following journals, in which versions of these poems have appeared:

Agni: "I Pray for No More Reagans"
The Alembic: "In the Valley of Too Much Rain"
Berkeley Poetry Review: "In the Blue Room"
Boston Review: "Students"
Boulevard: "Immortality Ode"
Crazyhorse: "Hart Crane: A Dream for Two Voices"; "Hart Crane: A Coda"
Grand Street: "Catullan," parts 4, 5, 8
Greensboro Review: "Afterbody"
Harvard Magazine: "His Father Waiting for the Light to Devour Him"
Harvard Review: "To the Executive Director of the Fallen World"; "To the
        Executive Director of the Actual"; "Catullan," parts 1 and 2
Kenyon Review: "February Sky"; "Drivin' and Cryin'"
New Virginia Review: "Lover and Ex"
The Oregonian: "Club Lament"
Painted Bride Quarterly: "Suite for the Possessed"; "His Father in the
        Exhaust of Engines"
Partisan Review: "The Clearing"
Pequod: "Stroke"
Poetry: "The Child We Didn't Have"
Salt Hill Journal: "A Living"
Slate Magazine: "Letter"; "1-A" (under the title "1-A, 1968")

Times Literary Supplement: "After St. Vincent Millay" (under the title
    "After Millay"); "Art"; "I'll Make a Broken Music, or I'll Die";
    "In Santa Croce"
Triquarterly: "After the Evening News"; "Delinquent"
Verse: "In the Absence of War"

A debt of immense and endless gratitude to Peter Balakian and Jack
Wheatcroft. And for the gift of the English Department at the
Putney School: Paula McLain, Harry Bauld, and Hugh Silbaugh.

For my students Casey Greenfield and Emily Gordon: "He most honors
my style who learns under it to destroy the teacher."

For Lucie, abiding.

THE OTHER LOVER

The Piano Lost in the Divorce

We love each other now
      as we loved each other then:
always and seldom. What's changed is the how
      and the why and the when.

Now one wants the heirloom endowed
      with purple, the hammers loud red
felt; the other wants what's owed
      on the *mortgage*: the pledge of the dead.

One wants what moved through the rooms like a nurse
      bringing something for a fever.
It made us howl. It makes us curse
      the family and the family's curse: money and power.

Too little money, and the power to hold
      a pedal down. The air sustains us.
It gives us something. It withholds.
      Now, the most heinous

acts we perform like a nocturne
      for two hands behind the back.
Art lovers: it's art and love that monster
      us and move us to take an axe

to the lid, then the keys and the hammers
and strings, true percussions
for the faithlessly wed, amateurs
of hate and its improvisations.

Afterbody

Catches and skips, scratches and cracks
along the edges, failures to be justified, to be exact,

a ghost slur, a quaver
and stop. From the most meager

scraps of voice on the telephone—
a half tone or quarter tone—

he pieces the body together: widow's peak, collarbones,
pelvic tilt, lobes and clefts, the body cloned

from some pressures and inflections,
a stammered word, interference, aspiration.

And in the background, the rip and hot patch
of heavy equipment, a greater rapture, pitched

to the lower registers of our hearing in a voice
that summons another body from the null and void

of now. Workmen, and a woman with a stop sign,
shout, I can hear them, their alignments.

It's crucial. It's water. There's a great thirst.
There's a need, a justified failure, a pipe burst.

Letter

Behind the door, cigarette smoke and perfume
move to embalm the world room by room . . .

in the first break from each other on the honeymoon,
sore, with a kind of horror-movie anticipation

of what's behind the innocent and beautiful,
still we want to have the face revealed

but not yet. She's on the other side,
fuming, he's on the other side, divided

by the pleasure of a hinged, hollow-core
door under which he wedges a letter

of his troth, and gets back
a letter with teeth marks and lipstick.

The mistake was opening, wanting more
than what could be had on paper.

Flight

I'm an accountable someone taxied down runways indicated
by small sapphires of light and contraindicated

by the city's heart condition, cataracts, and scum.
My inroads on the night are assisted by Valium

and are carried out at great heights by uniformed
men with well-modulated voices I've spent my entire life

to this belt-tightening, oedipal juncture hating. I'm off
and flawlessly yawed toward you, Miss Bliss,

that you may love me to *Beast of Burden*, or better,
Daddy, You're a Fool to Cry, with its emotionally sleek,

sympathetic identification with all those who strive, seek,
come home from work, sleep—slower for all those whose rock

and roll is dance of hurt and release, hurt and release.
A voice I don't believe tells me *our ground-time here will be brief.*

Art

We are living in Penns Grove, New Jersey, once again.
There is sand and once again the brine
and cabbage and gunpowder from the DuPont plant,
a nostrum so acid and uncertain
we don't know if it's distressed the time
past recognition or etched the solvents
like a Munch print on our faces. In one of these places
we rent, we live at the cul-de-sac's
puncture where some ugly breach
took place between the middle-management, sullen-faced
whites and the violently underclass blacks—
the DMZ we called it, the newlyweds. You teach
in the riotous schools, the delirium and honeymoon of art,
and the timeless, this is the sixties, deathless part.

I'll Make a Broken Music, or I'll Die

—Roethke

1.

If the four boiled men on my block
had speech beyond the wet *kiss*
from the imperfect embouchure
of their lips on the bottles of the shamrock-
emblazoned Tokay, and if this
emptied oil drum fueled by jilted furniture
could be their mouth, then they could sing
of the passing into darkness
with the perfect pitch and modulation
of silence and how it feels being
what's collected in the winds
and not the song.

Of the almost-songs we are, this
voiceless one is the loudest.

2.

It's in New York City I'm receiving the call
of the alto saxophone as I drop through the barrel
vault of the building to the street where the real

worship is being performed on the bearings
of the elevated body of the Lincoln Town Car
although I hear another greased parishioner prefers
the Eldorado, and then the same upper register
summons eight bars, nine bars later . . .

Sojourner Truth, this is for you
and the residents of your namesake apartments
at 106th Street across Columbus Avenue,
that we may always have this accompaniment
as our slave-song, god-song, and continue to burn
with the zeal of the internal combustion engine.

I Pray for No More Reagans

in the voice of Simone Weil.
I'm Emma Goldman's cousin
I tell them, I'm the gloves of Sugar Ray
Robinson when he fought Jake LaMotta
in 1951. Everyone remembers,
everyone applauds. I'm your next check, your butter.
I'm your watch, your gasohol, your future,
I tell humming them. I'm your slide into the upper
middle and beyond. I'm your parole and pardon
from the bank-prison, broom-prison. I'm your venture
capital, your steak, your 1000 islands.

So, I gave them a voice and they wanted a body.
I gave them a weapon and they wanted a prayer.
When I say "them," I mean nobody.
When I say nobody, I mean nobody.

Is it any wonder, then, he became a shadow?
His days dissolving and his nights corrosive,

but a thicker specter less innocent, less graceful
than the dead. He stumbled and fell, he scraped his knees

on the cement and bled. He became the shade
of ease and embarrassment, the ghost of his class—

the movie of a white boy running past . . .
Or like the woman whose white dress

passes at the upstairs window,
he writes, paints, plays the piano—

a maiden aunt lost in the expenditures
of notes and tempera and papers.

Later, he appears as a shadow boxer, a small
class struggle, a mad and fearful girl, a plural.

Delinquent

Sometimes the gun is pointed at the temples
when I want the silence its chambers can bring
and sometimes it turns itself on the evening
to shoot out the imperial street lights and the beautiful
neon in emotionally neutral cafés whose redolent
light is as difficult as smoke, as stammering
language to hold. Now I can be delinquent
in the dark, except for the star point flashing
from the neck of the broken bottle
on another century's mill dam in Lawrence,
Massachusetts, where I hear looms like axes grinding
with complaint into my temporary little hell.
The sound is like the sharpening of my pencil
I turn and point down and away from myself.

After the Evening News

"Lovers were not, Marina, are not permitted to know
destruction so deeply."
                                    —Pasternak to Tsvetaeva

I knew the face I used
to watch the young Columbian,
Omira Sanchez, die could not be used again.
While she was the bright event,
I was the impotent hindsight
from the voice-over announcement of an act of God.
She was neck deep in the mud
from the volcano's eruption and flood;
she was the buoyant face above,
and not an arm's length beneath, the embrace of
her grandmother's corpse. *What day is it?*
I'm afraid I'll miss my math test,
she said, and I kept watching the television
until I saw the New York Giants disfigure Washington.

Not once and forgotten like a man's
orgasm ten years, twenty years later.
Not twice or a third time—water
under something, wind
around. Not notches on the pearl-handled gun,
deed, date, the Kings and Queens
of England, G.I. crosses at Normandy, or the wings
of moths stretched and smudged above their Latin.

Not in history but in time. And not the bright moment—
red giant, nova, white hot star—
but the black gravity
of who you were,
Omira Sanchez, an eternity,
a mouth, a lover's mouth.

In the Blue Room

1. Just as I Had Signed Away My Life

in the event that I was held hostage
and learned to rat my way through the portals,
corridors, and locks of the penitentiary, I saw the last jags
of a man who had fallen and shrivelled into the fetal
position on the floor after drinking most of a tin
of duplicating fluid from the mimeograph machine.
He held himself and thrashed like a grunion,
waterless, on the granite of the B-wing tier of Education . . .

Later is a Babylon I write from where I can say
he failed to copy himself out and died a dull-purple,
pre-evolutionary thing. I write and rewrite his body
but fail the literal. No hammer, no will, no craft
can repeat the heart's distressed elegy,
our suicide note, the first and final draft.

2. Two Men, Rampant

On another day that is hermetically
preserved for me as if in tins, I could see
from a deep blue distance the fake Florentine tower

where the guards held guns, discreetly, and the power
of the architecture was to be archeology
every life held in its amber, in its prehistory
of stone, bronze, iron of the walls, shields, and locks
in which I found an exact measure of our lack
of civilization. I open to the day

in question, a beaten silver and hot.
The ruins I uncovered of the riot
were the heraldic figures of two men, joined at the hip,
head-locked, hunched, and white-lipped
and perfectly still in their grunts to kill each other.
They looked as if they were looking carefully down
for something lost in water.

Immortality Ode

Miss Bliss, once I thought I was endless
since father was perpetual in his grade school
of seedlings in cups, the overly loved pets, and recess
while mother was the lipsticked dancing girl
on the Steel Pier who would outstep Hitler.

I was insufferable when I rolled
the Volkswagen bus two times and lived
with the snow chains like costumed jewels
slung over me and the spare rolled
away as in a folktale.
The pact I made in the spinning instant
said in my language of American
boy, *Put up or shut up*, to God,
the State Trooper who was kind
and spoke of service and punishment
and giving yourself away.

Now, I'm alive through the agency
of iron and contract work and appeals
to the fallen—angel and dusk—
but wet-winged and still without you,

Miss Bliss, who took me inside
where there was an ocean
before which we were children.
That calm, that fear,
that witness of the two-thirds
of everything else.

Drivin' and Cryin'

The dogs stop their bark and listen.
The thirsty man stops and the man
in his wheel stops and the man stops

pushing his stone and listens, and the Furies
weep for the first time from the song
she sings along to, Bob Marley's

"No Woman, No Cry," where "porridge"
rhymes with "courage," this food
she takes in the places of fear,

in the vestibules and corridors of school,
in the rec rooms and dens, in the service elevators,
and in the cars breaking the silence of the kingdom

of the dead. She sings Public Enemy and Shanice.
She's receiving soul stuff, K-Solo, the Poor Righteous Teachers—
their agitprop, thrash, b-girl bop, foxcore—

voices like a dream notebook from Jung
and a page from the papers. It's a tribal yell
and a redundancy by which she lives. She lives

for the melancholy, the skank, the dead god's
odor in the trunk of the Olds. Her music is car crash
makeup for the corpse, its scratch

and break, three chords
and a death wish,
her spine vibrates

at each end—head and hips—until
she's bleeding and happy, foot
tapping and then doing the new dance.

The night opens. The punished
stop their punishments. The dead
love their saxophones

and the organ riffs and horns
of the girl Orpheus. It's an art
that hell welcomes—

sweet nothings and ruin,
rhyme and no regret. Music against harm
and harmlessness.

for Megan

His Father in the Exhaust of Engines

All his life I used my father
to get somewhere

else—the game, the shore, the power,
the color, the middle class, the other

side. When he bent over
the maw of the Ford—the generator,

the alternator, the plugs he muttered
motherfucker into, the sputter

and choke and dying spark—a fender
in one hand, a frayed wire

in the other, bent like a wanderer
in the middle ages before

a statue of the virgin—I swore
I'd never bow and scrap before

the orders. He swore
softly and finally, the R's

caught somewhere in the rivet and bloom
of the engine. A coughed *harom*

while we idled on the spur
of Philadelphia, America, nowhere

fast. A small purchase, a seizure
like what a moan and shudder

is from a man tortured
or bored or dying *la petite mort*

and I'm the son ignorant of motor
but prodigal of fuel and air.

I'm the emir of the four cylinder,
the chopped and channeled lord

of Detroit and Japan. I floor
it, my foot on his back, or,

his on mine, his face in the mirror,
his death doubling me over.

Double Sessions

Once I was crushed by the gift,
the privilege in late August in Pennsylvania
like Teresa in the wild dust of Avila
dry-mouthed, dilated, enthusiastic

with the nation in waiting. I was a war
baby with a burning in the wrists,
around the heart, a body ravished
by sport—that war-battered father

theater—the war made tenderly violent,
then property, then Yahweh. He made football
as a way to keep the many of us in thrall
to the hurt that made us indolent

little boys and fat men on the rich, clipped grass.
We must be punished for our skill.
We must be punished for Roosevelt and Churchill.
We bruised each other and patted each other's ass.

We covered the breastbone that permitted kissing.
We took two thousand showers.
We quartered and limited the hours
of a season like gods. What was missing

could be swiftly and surely achieved
if you wanted it,
if you wanted it
badly, more than your enemies—

those other boys who had risen
in the mist of late August
in other states to run in the locust-
loud double time of double sessions

as if we were a court or congress.
That time was crazed with fine lines
of our breaking into masculine
and feminine, an earth under duress.

1-A

I threw myself down the corridor
to fracture my skull or separate my shoulder—
to get out of the Army, but I was a coward.

To conscript the body of the boy,
I had to nurse the dying
and woo the nervous girl I was who cried.

I was of two hundred thousand minds,
one wavering one wanted to outlive
the Asian rain and wind

where the grasses were bent
by the rotors and I saw myself borne
on a stretcher with my organs.

Another mind wanted to die
for a body other than this specimen
I was, the body of the becoming one,

woman not yet beloved. If only
I could dent the dry wall
by running down the carpeted hall

of the apartment and show the draft board
the courage of my fear. Judge
and jury, I just wanted to be loved

or senseless, I could not not miss
myself, the yellow wall was my politics
and the pitch of my childhood's wish.

I ran as fast as I could, but I could not run
fast carrying the man I was like a pillow
so that I might suffocate my shadow.

His Father Waiting for the Light to Devour Him

He was puffed up with knowledge from the IVs
and from the failure of his kidneys.

He was a spoiled child, my mother said,
the firstborn, golden wings, golden head.

I could see the face of the dogface and grunt,
the soldier, in the creature the catheters and shunts

formed around him. It was the snake
of his father wrapped in the snake

of his mother. He was blue from the embrace.
In the cracks of his face

light, like the light from the first flash
of appearance—the world his wet nurse

and ash, his sweet cake and oven.
The war he served in

and its afterbirth preserved him
like a salty baby. Everything was in him:

his X and Y, his earth wrench, his star,
his spit in the ocean, his ruin, his for

a while. I remember being remembered by him:
the mouth, the sucrose, the fiery skin

of the child left out in the world
so long he spoiled.

Stroke

1.

The body's middle passage,
its Verdun, its Lost Continent, its Trail of Tears.
The private history without ecstasy,
what you can't compare . . .

2.

Outside the ward of cardiac and stroke,
a day of gray and lilac smoke
particular with rain, May First,
and work deferred for socialists,
work abandoned like the clothes
of lovers. Each blossom is a clot.

Body betrays the mind betrays the body.
In his room, he is mostly body
garlanded with wishes
from the children kept indoors for recess
who crayon hearts above the threshold and vision
of the spectrum for their retiring teacher,
this machine from the man, my father.

3.

It's a premature elegy—
there's half-life in the old man
yet, little sparks and charges in the brainpan
like broadcasts of ghost radio stations,
mostly static and hum, occasionally
a cough, a sucking through a vacuum, then
          "An elegant sufficiency" or
          "Jesus Christ . . . Dizzy Gillespie!"
and surges and purges of the blood
like a climax by de Sade.

4.

Little Bodhisattva in his gurney bed
wheeled and dreamed and received in the vein,
the measured sea, sugar, ampicillin—
the surrogate blood and ersatz godhead.

5.

After the War to end all wars,
the axis tilted in his direction,
the waters receded, the light brimming, the nation
muddy and warm, the fathers squint in the sun-

strafed Philadelphia and ask what will it be?
The family business huckstering plums and melons?
The Delicious, the berries, the persimmons,
the Big Boys, the scarlet runners, the parsley—

post-war flowers and brown-bagged possibility.
What was it, then, that wormed in him toward teacher?
What sky-voice said throw away the peach pit
he sucked on through the Great Depression's

Iron Age and look! Behind him! The new
soft, aspirant forms—slips and sprouts and honeydews
and sweet peas, the little ones, the children who
would need to be taught the new

Utopia of Montessori, Dewey, Piaget
from the small promontory of Summerhill.
He would be the philanthropic worker bee
in his green colony, in his glory.

      6.

On the outskirts of capital,
below the Mason-Dixon line,
on the freeway of Egypt and Mesopotamia,
Wilmington's a mute white man
held in the arms of the marginal.

He's the end of an industry vaguely Christian:
solicitous, efficient, redemptive, kind,
bureaucratic, censorious, doomed, and resigned.
From 9 to 5 in the hands of angry technicians.
I confuse the doctors and the dietitians.

He's a port for the sharp and the shining,
the father cut along his scars
and fixed with shunt and catheter
to let the old wounds flow again
with male milk, blood, and semen.

7.

My arms under his arms. I lift him, cross
chest, like the carry of a drowning victim,

to bathe him and shave the face that watches
me watch him, horror-face, bunker face,

mime-Christ, canvas and slash, clown-face,
shadow, mask over mask, the mannered face

of a man beached on the sheets he'll distress.
His instinct for instinct is endless.

Awkward at the shore, thirty years ago,
we let him sleep face down until the sea

rose to claim him and he awoke,
enraged, annoyed, then smiling at the joke

on him, shaking the foam from around his head
like a spaniel and shivering, the vacationing good

human being of Brecht with mouths to feed,
faces to imprint before the flood and ebb.

Eating the Man

The state took a big bite out of him
and the feds took a good chunk of the pensions.

The army grafted some of the tender skin
from his neck, and the navy got the mechanism

of the inner ear. Bosses inflamed
his joints, knee and hip, when he salaamed,

and the drive home made him scream and shake
like ten thousand applications of the brakes.

When I took my hand away from his mouth,
the scream was gone inside him. A sackcloth

of quiet around his form, his Xed form,
his dumb number, his unbecoming form.

I ransacked the face for shame and anger, for some
god, before I sat down to the beef of him,

the pasha's extravagant flesh
of the right side, the gristle and sinew of the left

from the stroke. The ribs gave up the sweet,
lip-glistening grease. I sucked my teeth

and the long bones for the marrow.
He was a sweet creature for a man of sorrow,

although I had to boil the heart, like chitlins,
for three days and still it was a man's

fist clenched against the masculine, but
it's one more the state won't get.

In the Absence of War

Today I will eliminate all the causes of war
from my life, beginning with the rancors
against the president and the other impresarios
of power who promise to kick some ass and do so
in my name. I will eliminate my name.
I will speak softly and eliminate the stick. I'll dream
small and often. I'll parry the thrust.
I will conduct my intolerance like lightning into the earth.
I will swallow a toad each morning for breakfast
so that the rest of the day may taste
less bitter. I will jilt the lover
in me of petty advantage, bigoted favor.
I'll limit my death without becoming the killer.
Sure I will.

Students

You see me here smeared
with chalk and pressed against
the slate-gray triptych from fear,
white as paper, white as a flensed
seal. Sometimes I can step outside
myself and listen
to my voice in its best bedside
manner reassure with glistening
lies, with cool purgatorial lies,
that although this is fall
we are not complying
and my heart goes out to myself.

I think when I go home of the syllabus
of love and horror movies
you've sat through in the Very Rich Hours
of your summer. The corpses are gorgeous,
and the books just begin to be
the artifice we need to begin.
To begin: *to cut open*. To love:
to be cut open and to heal and to cut open.
And I thought I could be above
it all—professional, textual, sacrificial.

Epaulette

After her death I kept finding her hair
sutured through a sweater or
braided in the shoulder of a coat
like the officer's "scrambled eggs"—
the insignia of an army
that marches on the stumps of its legs.

Groove and Break: His Voice at Fifty

I.

There were do-it-yourself kits they assembled, my parents,
     and stained a maple and varnished and steel-wooled
and varnished. It would be our style—reproductions
     of the old and valuable, the American primitives,
worked on, worked up. Having no past, my mother made my father
     stop for a dry sink or a deal on a hutch. The warped boards
of the table meant the blood from the roast collected
     on my plate like a stroke at five o'clock,
a puddle in the lower lobe. *There was plenty*
     for some families. For us, family hold back and can't
complain for others had seeds, starch from a box,
     and bark-peeling, baby-strangling hunger.
I learned quiet and eat, speech as mastication, too many
     syllables, a mouth full, or outside, the growl
of a mongrel and snap at its own balls, maybe fleas, maybe
     the soul in torment in paradise he guarded, curled
back on himself at the entrance to the gates of Philadelphia,
     nineteen-fifty, I'm four, and the dog must have had the mange,
and in the rabid itch and fang and bark at nothing
     but itself, a voice that is my birthright.

2.

And always the music that was not my own
        beyond the bore of engine and the El's metal on metal,
the boy's heart, not my own but a bristling thing,
        like a pine cone or the fur of an animal
that would carry the spoors out by wind
        or friction. From the basement, uncle with a highball,
wrists blue from work in the chemical plant
        listening with the attention of the working stiff
to his death. He who must sharpen himself to pierce
        the off-hours and dull himself to forget the hemorrhage
of work. La Traviata it was, the fallen woman whose throat
        pulsed in his temples and solicited sleep.
Upstairs, a baby alligator in a tank uncle brought back
        from Florida. It snapped at pencils and ground beef
and thunked its tail when it would turn over or turn into
        something at night. For the boy, two minds: I/he,
the hi-fi and the reptile behind glass—both pink-mouthed
        and cat-eyed and thickening silently. I slept with a radio
like the sister I never had who whispered through the transistor—
        a maroon unthrown brick through a window—
the frequencies of black singers, a groove I'd tunnel through
        into oblivion. Said: *Ooo, child.* Said: *Take me, Shake me.*
Said: *Just another little piece of my heart, now Baby.* Bleeding
        through the grid, the horns, the goatskin and wood, the scream
that snatched my body and in its place left the mute who heard
        the city as hum and hiss.

3.

I listened in the Valley of Too Much Rain,
        where the orchids were pink-mouthed divas,

for my voice. I listened in the climax forest
        and in the anechoic chambers of old growth.
I heard the muzzy barge horns coming down the gorge,
        burr and drawl of log trucks, April,
and the rain like the singers with their cargo
        of legato and bliss. I heard my voice
in the beloved's and it was a hound that wanted out
        of the body, or *beside or above*, anywhere
the spirit was. I heard a howl and a child's cry,
        a father stitch, a mother scald, the voice
of the coach on loss. I spoke with the voice of the mistress
        of the vernacular, the house slave singing,
in code, her charms. Others had their talk around the table,
        their stories, like light they'd carry with them
into the next life. I woke from the dream, mud
        and winged things, grunts and green visions,
betrayals, and I knew how to spit.

        4.

Brilliant outside. The window a voice. Red a C,
        F a pale green, G is blue. Silver the groove,
black the breaks. The world said something
        I could only know by choking back
all that was not me, my hands at my own throat,
        the voices rising, the gorge rising, coughing up
all the woman in me to speak silently
        the chewed-on, midweek song of the dying.
Friday, payday. Saturday, the bridge
        between the ash and the resurrection. Said:
Can you take us to the bridge?—James Brown
        to his saxophonist who used the ax

to split my tongue. Uncle dreams of blue veins in the throat,
       the aria of broken light in his shot glass.
(The lizard in the glass was my ventriloquist.)
       Said: *bliss is what disturbs*. Said: *lips
are wounds*. Said: *Who's on bass?* Said:
       There is always a mad dog defining with his bark
one end of speech, the other end a voice
       in the reluctant embrace, tremors, catches,
and this is my tongue.

Living After All

Kafka: "One cannot not-live life after all." A modest sainthood then, enduring
everything caught up in its Not. Not paradise. Not loss. Not self. Not quite other.
Vivas to those who are equal to one another by their wounds of castration.
I would be eunuch to my desires were it not for the lizard in me, the
nocturnal, lidless creature able to grow back what's lost . . .

One writes *in* English. As if language were a room to break and enter,
careful to check for the exits. One can be silent in a language, too.
One can be possessed *by* it—those foreign, almost sexual differences—but
never really possessing it. It's a tongue that licks and heals.
Never master, never culture, a conditional music. Like wolves
offering up the throat to the other—submissive, obedient,
resigned. I give up. Here's my throat. The gutturals are
apologies in my animal voice for the sadness, the soreness of living
after all. I spoke and it was all wrong, but not unloving.

Suite for the Possessed

Miss Bliss, in Penn Station during its renovation, dust and draped masonry, waiting for velocity multiplied by distance over time. Flickering arrivals into and from the classical dome and vault. The simple distance. Light. An occasion for belief in *The Patriot, The Limited*. A beefy officer rouses the dispossessed.

I was looking at everything in the other's face: shining thing, baby, Shiva dancing, skin, the fetish of lip, lash, the eye and its socket, necrophilia and will: the voodoo of two thousand years.

We're beside ourselves with belongings like bastard children, firstlings, fatlings, attachés and rucksacks, a crushed homunculus, red vanity, luggage duct-taped like the mouth of a hostage, a pouch like a cyst, money belt, reliquary. We're not where we want to be.

I was wild. I was banging. I loved heroine. I did whatever. I went to this place and worked all night bagging. I come home and had a lot of hundred dollar bills. I used to use the vein in my neck. Any vein I could find in my body.

The other says legs wrapped around specifically you. Entering and being entered. Like Poland, love me like Hitler loved Poland.

Down the steps to the coaches in the pearly light. We used the windows to shoot the buffalo. Now there's no end to the horizon, to the silvered motes of other people's lives seen from behind their trees and clouds, barrels and drums, their industries and weeds.

A voice in Esperanto is from somewhere via the boroughs announcing the cosmos expanding and contracting. It's transmitted in that stressed, unstressed voice that seems to move us, the language a wheel.

Miss Bliss, gods and goddesses mingle their muscle with apple blossom and breath of mortals. One body is held by the wrists. In this way a nation is made. Then salt and belongings. Then you can't feel what it's like to be specifically you.

A dream: Boston to New York via Sparta and Athens. I'm armed, you're naked, a demon on each shoulder. You're violent with words: poems, curses, songs, news. You spit in the firebox of the engine. I'm mute pumping the hand truck like Buster Keaton. One track, one way. I'm slow, murderous, smoky in the soft coal of my rage. You're swift and efficient; the wheels spark and squeal. Nobody can stop it: the demon the angel this collision we're headed for. Why can't they cushion it with a body of silence, a body of words?

Hart Crane: A Dream for Two Voices

Rummaging through a trunk

     I moved from Cleveland to New York City

in the attic of my old 115th Street place

     to Brooklyn to Cuba back to the country

looking for something the dark

     where I sang and danced then to Paris and Mexico City

dimly seen trove of my mother's things lace

     and the god of pulque but I could not move away

slips and shimmies a bandeau a rose ensemble

     Things of hers letters I could abstract

stockings a shoe a peignoir

     a sad heart from a tongue-lashing and lips

in white streaked with red I empty it and it stays full

     puckered enraged with the self-shuddering fact

too full to find whatever it is I'm looking for

     her son the homosexual. A sailor slim-hipped

Then I feel a hand and then another

     Apollo in gob blue I wanted but I could not be filled

and then a piece of an arm within a negligée

     I remember the rats bloated with typhus

a corset, a bloody gown, bloody under-

     in the bright night water off Vera Cruz it chilled

things everything bloody sticky

     and sickened me like the D.T.'s like the orchids

with blood but not until this moment do I know the body

     of Baudelaire whose self I am

I unpack oh mother woman baggage parcel of agony

     And I am Kit Marlowe I am Christ I am Whitman

To the Executive Director of the
Fallen World:

I count my white life as one of the fallen into Earth-minus-America, as if it were desert, river, mountain, and the sky voice still thundering . . . As if I were I and not a stammer in the name of others. As if the wind were innocent.

For nine days I fell. It was like being fondled by God. I had speed instead of God's bright, precious time. It wasn't pride that had me glazed and fired; it was an urge like gravity, like seed to cervix. Then I was plural: We, Us, my body and the bodies of the Also Fallen. We share a fate as we share a mouth. We crossdress—her yoke, my ruffle. We kiss—my longing, her fear. We circulate like cash.

Angel of Coma, Angel of Capital, Angel of Gnaw Your Own Bone, Angel of Fetish for the Thing, Angel of Stomach, Angel of Virus, Angel of Forgetfulness.

Director, I beat my wings to cool the machine and sing the field hollers of *when* and *why*. I have slang and the late century's dialects—Security and Catastrophe—as my tongues. My eye is artifice, my ear's experience, my life's the music of too many notes: Big Bang, baby boom, then a mute over the proletariat, Europe smothered in hard bop, growl and grunt, the sound of an engine turning over, the click of the keys to the kingdom, whatever *Please Please Please* made its way like x-rays through my skin, and gunshots real and replayed, echoes of gunshots, the spent cartridge falling on the pavement, the new round in the chamber . . .

I still hear the rumors of heaven. They speak to me still—Angel of Small Arms Aimed at the Heart, Angel of You and What Army Can Stop Me, Angel of Pay and Pay, Angel of Give It All Away.

When I fell, the air around me was like a scalding. And gravity a judgment separating the damned and the saved. I did not flap my wings. I fell. I spiraled down like your maple seed, your autumn. I kept my hands still like dead wrens and swallowed the yell, so that I'd shatter into the hundreds of me—each cell a voice, each voice an agitated call—or I'd fall as the steer falls becoming beef and from my nose a worm of blood, pupa of the New Thing.

Angel of Rough Trade, Angel of Diesel, Angel of Rat Fuck, Angel of Forget It.

Everywhere is Times Square or Sunset Boulevard: the glut and the look, the overheated and the sleeping. A glass jar with flowers shattered in the street. Our terrors and promises frozen in the architecture like a deer drawn in stone. Even the restorations, the arteries and the projects, are made from someone's blues and ashes and sentiment.

Director: Your crack, your rage, your work and childbirth, your cars and harvest songs—your forms of not God are what we are: Angels of the Verifiably Beautiful, and beneath that The Beautiful, and beneath that The Skull, and beneath that The Beautiful.

To the Executive Director of the Actual:

Is this the world, Miss Bliss? Stacks of ingots on the docks where my brother works? Work and things on the threshold of raw and radiated. Bananas gassed in shacks to ripen by the forklifts. Ships of foreign port. Ships of car parts and dyes. The beef-stripping business. Things, Miss Bliss, and work. Flavors translated from Costa Rica, volatile oils, seized cargoes, incensed loads, cracked coal. After a week the exposed skin around his wrists was blue, vein color, the color of the world. Labor, and the union of the senses to deliver us from our geography. Everywhere is here.

When the stevedores break for lunch, one is responsible for the pot-luck of cold meats, the deep dish, leftovers from the wedding, while one is responsible for inviting the office women. These men set the table with the pomp of the late Elizabeth: linen, gilt plates, a taster, and a trumpeted summons. They force the choice bits on each other. They talk about blood and Solomon's operation. They talk about Lily's kids and the dead as they come back to speak to Lonnie in his sleep. And they talk about food they could not eat, the boss, and a dream of playing lead before they switch on the TV with its loud prophecies of soap. They eat deeply in gratitude. The pot scraped with a spoon, that sound. The world's a word, and a lever.

The ghosts at the banquet want something, Miss Bliss. From one world I come to you with two blue wrists, my brother's rage against the living the world owes, and everything I do that's duplicate. My cells split. They can't be true. I smoke. I turn out a little verse. I make a small sacrifice. I throw what cannot be eaten away. I throw it on the ground. Here, some things you can't eat.

Memory of Italy

Etruscans were bone-brown lizards.
Etruscans were cool tombs and dust

where the German cameras whirred.
You held your breath all over

the nation you dove
and surfaced in, little American, like a passion

flower for Columbus in the New World.
In the Old World, obstetrical tools

and orrery of the Medici in the museums—
gilded overkill. The dead did not amuse

you or their resurrection, too much
sun, too many zeros in the money.

You opened for the Roman cats
who nursed your fingers, famished Romulus

and Remus, and again on the train
for the soldier who folded and unfolded

origami swans. Where is the mother?
the conscripted asked. A harried father

took your hand by accident in Venice.
Our rooms were darker museums

where I lost and lost in the hands of five-card draw
all the beautiful coins we used to call home.

Lover and Ex

Everything is everything, the bebopist says.
In the Tuscan summer, my skin,
my sweat, my shadow, the olive grove,
its skin, its sweat, its shadow.
I walked in the mid-ground
in a stillness so still you knew
someone had finished playing
or the first breath just taken, lips to reed,
before beginning and you
open because here comes the fire,
the dying race and the cool water.

Later, at the café, everyone had loved
one another—*tu* and *Lei*—and they stood
in their quavers and rests and slurs,
lover and ex-lover, some held, some struck,
some carried. We must be accurate
about the peach pit on the table—
a tiny human heart and the light
was a rash. We went our ways.
Art is no river and no Rome.

Club Lament

Dark spots and spotlights on the stage,
a rouged smog behind the bar
where a white light is bent over
the cash register in a tiny funnel
like a calla lily.
The televised girl and the real girl
whose work is her form as if being
were a job plus tips and sometimes
a ten folded like a scout tent
and left as a largess.

Brown and cream buffed skin
that's a thorn in the hands of the men
and demands that they put their mouths
to the meat of their thumbs and suck.
Or they drink and wipe their brows
and don't blink.

The closeness and the distance.
Six inches away, six inches near.
A light-year from someone he loved
for a minute.

Above the pulse of the three minutes of flash
and ax work of the bass guitar, the decorum
and trespass, the ambush of the light,
the women move
on the stunning points
of their heels.

The Child We Didn't Have

has your broad shoulders and my weak eyes.
She's blessed with her mother's face
while she has my stumpy limbs and lack of grace,
and in her fretful unborn sleep the sighs
I won't be disturbed by are not her strangulation,
crib death, asphyxiation, fever, seizure, paralysis.
There will be no sympathetic pangs, no morning sickness,
no clipped umbilicus,
post partums, blues, shocks of separation

except the one we made the last day. If this is
not the exact transcription, this is close
enough as to be admissible evidence. Let it be said
I slept in the fetal position on the floor
near the space heater, you occupied the space in the bed.
You get to keep the house, I get to keep the kid.

In Santa Croce

the world's greatest struggle for favor
goes on and I have been chosen
at this moment next to the monumental bones
of Dante—the real bones are in Ravenna—
to remember your ribs, your sacral hair, your shoulders.
It's a gorgeous view to be arched
and vaulted hard in your arms and to peer over
and down to where my five fingers
inform the chapel and blank mural of your back.

Pardon me, please, for making a woman's body
a sight to behold and forgive this wooing
that continues through marble and the more lordly
forms of acquisition, ransoms for the ensuing
exile from this land. In hell I will be blind.

Catullan

1.

Godlike but like the gods
in Madame Tussaud's—
most feared and loved
effigies—he sits at her side
catching her laughter and sighs
and makes a history,
a cozy mythology,
that drips down her thighs.

2.

I hate his great American name,
Hippolyta, the name of a city,
a capital! in the Midwest
in which power plants
burn first my arms and legs,
then my heart
and there you are
with him
in the electricity of me.

3.

Why don't you spare me
your "honesty," Hippolyta,
and your "love," now
that you tell me he
tickles you and you laugh.
He's dying
to get it up to prove
he's not dying.
We're all dying,
that's the smell you smell,
not the pulp mill.
He's crying
over my corpse—you love
him for this—
that you kick, then patch
it all up—like the leaks
in your yacht
which sails on the oil-
spilled sea of self-justification
under the winds of self-gratification.
It takes almost an hour
to circumnavigate your soul.
Love is a week wide
and six inches long.

4.

No matter how many pillows
you stick under that ass of yours,
Hippolyta, when you're fucking him,
and no matter how many zeros

in the price of the show horse
you'll name with the care of a poem,
you'll be the elevated whore
in your jackboots and breeches,
your crop, ten hands high, riding
what he can afford
saddled in the victimless
crime of your lying . . .

5.

Too much or not enough.
The blade-thin letter
from you, Hippolyta,
cuts nothing
not even the wrists.

Stop, I've had enough,
I imagine the letter
says. Or *I was wrong. Hippolyta.*
Or it says *Nothing*
you say makes these wrists

come back to you. Enough
is never enough. The letter
I don't read, Hippolyta,
I send back. Nothing
but a stamp. Slit your own wrists.

6.

The mess you left,
Hippolyta, shit
in piles like the Augean stables

Hercules had to muck.
On the rug, on the walls,
in the bed, your shit.

Pathetic, that I track it
everywhere, and they think
it's mine. They sniff
the air and check
their soles and stare. Pathetic
that I like the stink,

reminds me of your hair
tangled in my crotch
the morning after you'd gone.
I'd unknot it,
the long blonde strand,
and I'd smell my hands.

7.

Don't think I wouldn't have you back
in a heartbeat, Hippolyta, your face
shiny with his cum, creased from the sack.
It would be the privilege of my disgrace
to feel, by proxy, his cock
on my lips as I kiss you,
although now my heartbeat
is set to the work of eternity.

8.

I'm done subtracting three
hours from the time of day

to find how the light
strikes you in the West, Hippolyta.
Early or late. You're asleep
next to him. I'm up.
Or I'm thrashing in my sleep
night sweat, no dream,
you're offering three
orifices to him.
Leave me out of it.
Subtract one.
Stick a fork in my ass.
I'm done.

9.

Hippolyta, you could be black-eyed
and fat in your seventh month
with you-don't-know-whose kid
and begging for bus fare
that you'll use for crack
on the streets of Rome
and I would not, or would,
after the appropriate gesture,
give you the change.
But what is the appropriate gesture?
To tell you your high horse
is glue, now, and the pity
is my luxury, your necessity?
And then I would turn away
into the shadow of myself.
And then I'd put my eyes out.

The Clearing

When the men on the wards had medicated themselves against self-
felony and slept under their restraints, when the women
beaten by their men beat themselves into little slips
of things. When the LSD was licked from the envelopes

and the gun was smuggled—spring, trigger, and magazine—
into the ambivalent hands. One man said: *A gun with a bullet*
ought to separate the real Messiah from the impostors,
before he put it in his mouth. I thought of Faust,

skeptical in med school—no resurrection, no way out
of the body—before he became the soul's Rothschild.
One woman said: *I'll peel off my face with a razor*
in order to find the one under the one that won't kill

or be killed. Until then, Thorazine, lithium, and a dozen
purple hearts. When they were all under, when they were id
and superego, buzzed, unstrung humans, when they were cuffed
and chemically graced—Drugs are the jealous god—

I saw therapy was a sleeve
for their bleeding hearts,
their bleeding gums, their whacked and wounded
genitals, pressure sores, phantom wounds

dressed and drained. Out of their mouths, like a lit cigarette
the soul would burn and cloud. Their heads were unscented
flowers—all seed and sex. I'd sniff them, but
I'm professional, you know. It was then she came to me:

the tortured girl, my whipped shadow, my patient
impatient self. My initial diagnosis—an acute
someone suffering herself. Then the thousand iridescent
veils removed and rent. Her Viennese hands, her Florentine feet—

this was the Europe I made of her as we sat
in hard chairs and breathed. I dreamt I was seized
like a nipple by a mouth. A man can dilate,
can't he? A man can receive.

This was our romance, making a third body
both chaste and sexy. I'd forget myself then remember
the romantic sees the mad as suffering the truth,
the truth was the romance was killing me.

It can couple and blood. It can woo and work
its placebo effect. And I was afraid my desire was an open wound,
my mind a membrane between her
and the turbulence. I sensed her tremors

and fugues, yet I was distant, as if in a book—
a love story by von Clausewitz.
I saw that love's not shudder and sentiment
anymore than the racket on the wards at night—

the call and response—is the rhythm and blues.
She said: *That's the rain, I could be the rain.*
It's a terrible thing for a girl to be the rain.
She became my Crazy Jane and I was the thing

to be torn, the way one might unravel the spiral
of the double helix from the stem of our self.
I was a mess. An emotional petite mal,
my self-diagnosis. For five years I was in the furnace,

the wine press before we could dream an end.
I dreamt of wolves: a limb bit off, a cord chewed through.
I saw her vanish into the Rorschach of the world,
hues and saturations of her, those solids

and voids of the Actual with its *fade to black* and *jump
cut*. She sits in the room and becomes otherworldly
at dusk, it's like trying to touch perfume as she *fades
to black*. *Jump cut:* I'm in Vermont, sleepless

before the night's open spaces. The moon's an orange, open
wound. Still and clear. I get good reception. Talk
Net, the news, two cuts from "Kind of Blue"—that threshold
between cool and new. I can't step out of the world without it.

It soothes me, this necromancy, in stereo,
blah, blah, easy listening and dread,
it doesn't matter. I love the vacant embrace, shadow,
ion, grace note. I can't be Faust without it.

Sometimes the autistic panic from the changing shapes
of clouds. They want eternity with bounds, they want it
now. Heaven's four beats to the bar and no cheating,
otherwise heaven's another name for the pit.

It was difference not divinity I wanted.
I wanted a lesser violence, a lesser love.
She wanted the body worshipped, it became clear
to me, for its halo of hair and its limp from the wrestle

with angels. Desire is a shitty little history,
our regret, our art. *Fade in:* A man sleeps
after the nightlong seance with the radio. He dreams
a penis is grafted to his ribs and he's bleeding.

He wakes to fields radiant with rain,
Bindweed, Bitterweed, Everlasting,
the edges of the meadow electrified for horses
and the long-lashed, moon-eyed, Brown Swiss.

Clipped timothy and sweet grass, a man
can receive. A man can be received. She wanted clear
distinctions between herself and the rain,
it became clear to me.

East of Eden

Easy for you to say my name in the cool heaven of your skin while
spooning the other, licking, speaking in tongues, showing your scars
to him where the apple left the stem. Naming the body's Eden: he's
adam, you're Rib with Chomsky's politics. I'm experience or
serpent. I'm not god or I would kill with the righteousness of U.S. foreign
policy. I'm disarmed without you. I'm deaf and mute like capital Him,
although I still see the new boy in his khaki. I've imagined him out of
love turned violent. Like Cain sent *East of Eden*. He's James
Dean, you're the sensitive girl who can understand the pain.
I'm everything father, unforgiving, the failed experiment, I'm
Nothing until the named thing nameless is and is destroyed.
God, I miss you. Send me a scent, a sign that however much you
Love in your post-colonial winter, you'll shudder from the sight of
me, like some do the flag, the other, the snake making words beginning with S.

Dawn of the Dead

Dreaming of you *making love* to him—a dream with a
euphemism. Please don't let it be 4:41 of a stalled, blue-black
night in February in New England. *Dawn of the Dead* dubbed
in Spanish. No horror like the present. The end of us in color.
Sickening, gruesome, disgusting, cruel, crafted, funny, savagely drool.
Earth is the place where the dead walk when there's no room in hell.

Oh for a Virgil in this circle for those Who Loved
Someone Only to Betray the Heart. They need to be eaten, their need like
the dead is awful and pure, while the survivors are
ripped from within by greed, their dissatisfied shopping.
Only the scream is the same in both languages, the staged pain.
We're voyeurs of our end. The spilled seed of a dead letter signed
X for the crucifixion of St. Andrew, the lost slave name, the kiss
off, O for the empty embrace, the mouth I will miss, I guess.

A Living

1. September

"Once it was summer and the flies died
trying to find something to stick their infinite eyes to
and the insects let off steam, mid-afternoons,
before the rains came slowly and dyed
everything a deeper hue. It was the end of bliss
and the beginning of some comfort with its entourage
of nap and soup, its gentle disease. It took courage,
then, to remain hysterical and vain, soft and distempered
as the ripening-overnight tomatoes, melons, and peppers.

And they said *nothin'* when they arrived at school
about the months of glistening and ripping out the seams
of the baked neighborhoods in their parents' Chevrolets,
except, maybe, *unbelievable*. It was fall
and all they could say of their return to the world
was *unbelievable*.

2. My Charges

"Whatever era we're in, whatever undertaking,
I'm their bookish other, annoying, post-historical.
I'm the odor in their rose-scented yearnings.

They'll be shocked one morning—the white fireball
coming across the asphalt at them—into remembering
the gratuitous praises and humiliations of their schooling.

One's bouncing a check, one's nursing a baby,
one's got the figures for the first quarter's earnings,
one packs a bag for Paris, one joins the navy
for tattoos, one lives with Mother in antiseptic rooms,

when they discover the marred and discarded text
whose margins have the sketch of the bridegroom
without the bride and the indelible names of the ex-
lovers beside the vaginal and phallic signs
of their innocent and vanished tribe.

"For C. whose face was the face of the young Antigone.
For H. whose face was the face of many felonies.
For L. who wanted Princeton. For J. who got Fort Dix.
For N. who wanted the world fed and got local politics.
For D. whose love was a hunger starved all summer.
For T. to whom all corpses were familiar.
For S. whose music was MegaDeth and violin.
And for A., the heir to civilization.

L. thought of herself as a desk drawer,
the shallow purgatory of clips and receipts
that wait with the glues and the spores
for heaven or other people, in their dim recesses
like a squid in its ink. I want to be famous
each one thinks, and for M. who wakes from codeine
and takes an incomplete.

3. Love

"It's not that I love them
so much now, it's just that I hate
what I know they'll become. The sons—
thugs. The daughters—sons. Vice presidents of what
professions yet to be invented I can't imagine—
money plumbers, joiners, adjusters of air, death-pact
actuaries . . . What they profess to me is the cat/
doggish immediacies of sleep and eat a good bit
of what I feed them—the facts, just the facts,
as Sergeant Joe Friday said on *Dragnet*.
None of them have ever seen it.
Have you ever seen what they choose to be remembered by
in their yearbook's Last Will and Testament?
Even the most subtle, the most astute, select the deadly
scraps of fuck all and futureless sentiment.

4. Profession

"I believe passion can be learned
that you can prepare for it like the SAT's.
I consider myself a missionary to the suburbs,
and my mission is to instruct in the capacity
for fear and the ecstasy that comes from being bound.
It will take a really long rope,
I'm afraid, of great strength and expense to loop around
the heads and hips of them all. I hope
to wound each one of them before they become
less tender, destined, and armed. I mean to show them
films of wave motion and crematoria,
and they'll grab ass and be bored in the back of the room,

I know, when I darken it, sophomoric
as always, but the speech they will use as they emerge
from the dark will be mute to the inhuman and slurred.

"Everyone I know is terrified:
Tunnels and bridges, viruses and knives, neutrons loosed
into the asphyxiating bag of atmosphere. And the body—
shocks of hair uprooted, a digit removed, and the low-level *j'accuse*
of yourself, the survivor. There's a burning
I go through without the blister and cinder, without ash.
There's a shame, How Dare I?, concerning
my concern for myself. You see what a noose
it is. The secret is the children won't redeem us.
I was a child once and I was afraid
under the mother quilt and the sign of Aquinas.
Now, I'm the sister whose dread outweighs
her faith and reason, still I can teach
them my trembling, my obedience.

"When we burnt our fears
in my roasting pan on the last day of class
the fumes choked us. We opened the windows
wider and sat on the sills with our pencils and gasped.
That's my fear—to be left each year in sorrow
and pity, some fumbled thanks, a soap (a soap!)
to cover the odor, I suppose. I wanted fans
instead of charges, indiscriminate, heliotropic
plants aching in my direction. When they ran
fearless out in each other's arms, I dumped the ashes
and picked at a few blackened scabs on the bottom
of the pan. They want nothing but to pass

like light through these windows, a flash
through the aperture, and that's it. Next year in my kitchen
amid the sauces and smears of my other life,
I'll show them the oven.

5. A Job

"I was a teacher because I needed
that form of love daily, disfiguring,
flushed and edgy boredom, hormones transfiguring
the bodies of the equally needy.
And I loved one hundred of them, that is to say,
I walked in vaguely illuminated rooms of twenty-
odd and otherworldly, worldly, squeamish know-nothings
five times a day. Born after Kennedy, born after King.
Gangs of Aprils with the ice floes of January
and February still on their faces, faces ruddy as buds
and not one of them unlovely.
This was love.
This was a mindless, but not a heedless crush,
an exchange of ignorance, a sea change, rubs and rebuffs.

6. The Wooing

I

"I loved one.
A boy who sighed when we read 'To Autumn.'
Then I began to look back at him, right in his eyes,
brown, beneath hair like Shelley's.

And I watched his intelligent thighs
crossed when he sat in the corner or uncoiled at the bell.
He wrote a paper for me on 'Emily Brontë
and Passion,' headstrong and heartfelt, funny
and misspelled. All wrong, finally. But
I wanted him to know I'd lose my judgment
for him. I wanted a sign
that he understood my position, like a line
copied, anonymously, from Keats or Dickinson.
He waited until the grades were in.

11

"He wrote me breezy, English epistles—Browning to Barrett—
from college where he learned irony
from Shaw, distance and ambiguity
from 'the Masters'; and his dreams. I'd forget
myself with mine, 'the second life,' Nerval called it,
saying things without saying them. We would relive
this way each nuance and glance, a high literary pas de deux.
I wanted to tutor and seduce
and be seduced, wasn't this romance,
something out of Proust?

Did you think it would end up in other ways than dumb and blind
with regret? We met and he admitted he never understood
what I was getting at, *La Belle Dame* and all that.
I never could tell him just what I thought.
I said, I just want to fuck my brains out.

"OK, I wanted my mouth all over his.
I wanted the words with him
above me, and beneath me, him.
And teeth, and sleeping like spoons and waking, lips
parted and him inside me again.
Do you understand what inside
is for me? How it's the mansions inside
the house, like those Russian dolls, or the nucleus inside
the atom, ad infinitum, how it is really me inside
of him and nothing alien, passive, exclusively,
imperially him . . . I'm a woman who says forget
his gender. I want this one specific cock
inside of me and all that weight on top.
It's not even sexual, really.
My anatomy is his destiny.

IV

"I lost him,
the sophomore, the little shit.
Or I left, however you may want to put it.
Leaving is my real profession.
First, the story goes, it was commitment without discernment,
that is: idolatry, that is, I loved him!
Then it was discernment without commitment,
that is, Tartuffe, the crime of passion
lost, the sham of loving: hypocrisy. *Teaching
is the only profession*, Roethke said,
that permits love. It's a living,
I say, an act of kind and unkindness, a cooperative fraud.

At best dismemberment, at worst an avocation.
It's a loss for which there's no compensation.

7. Ten Things I Would Have Told Him If He Had Listened

1. The flies came back with their infinite eyes
      and wheeled around my head.

2. I wanted a baby or memory, not July
      thick, intemperate, inbred.

3. The *lune d'absinthe* follows the *lune de miel*.

4. After this labor, I'm closing again.

5. I wanted to get beyond the he and she
      of it, mishap of our cells and cherubim.

6. I wanted to know and not know the boundaries
      (like in Brontë, dig me up and fuck me).

7. It's just not four buttocks on a stem, a teaspoon of semen

8. You were the contraband I smuggled;
      you won't be held like that again.

9. I'm older. I'm smarter. I'm closer to tears.

10. Call me, no, write me a letter, in ten years."

After St. Vincent Millay

When I saw you again, distant, sparrow-boned
under the elegant clothes you wear in your life without me,
I thought, No, No, let her be the one
this time to look up at an oblivious me.
Let her find the edge of the cliff with her foot,
blindfolded. Let her be the one struck by the lightning
of the other so that the heart is jolted
from the ribs and the rest of the body is nothing
but ash. It's a sad, familiar story
I wish you were telling me with this shabby excuse:
I never loved you anymore
than I hated myself for loving you.

And about that other guy by your side
you left me for. I hope he dies.

In the Valley of Too Much Rain

She's   He's

        falling in the huge V

          chosen death by hanging

in the valley of too much rain

          after the crushing limbo of death row,

all the cells brimming and falling

          through the trapdoor

at the constant rate of gravity

          a greased rope around his hooded neck

and light which slows as the universe

          dropped into the air

expands in the valley of too much rain.

A slow erotic choke

Arms do what arms do

      crushing the windpipe, gasping

holding and letting go, falling

      from all his weight.

In the valley of too much rain

      He wants to grab the noose

falling and flailing hands and wave

      before it tightens too much

goodbye but not before the clench

      and not an instant sooner

unclench as if rising for a breath

      no breath, and he comes as if

held underwater, the air

      finally fucking nothing

soaked from too much rain

      finally everything

falling then reaching for a body,

      Ex: -felon or -lover, broken

anything, a limb in the dark green world

      man who would die—

to stop the falling in the valley

      anything to be another body

of too much rain and then still

      with the heaviness, the weight

falling, then finding wings.

Hart Crane: A Coda

Cold

    Cold

One syllable

    World

on the tongue

    I flail

then the cruel bottom

    my farewells

of the sea ten fathoms

    Beside myself

down where the dead

    I can listen

have read

    to the ocean

my poetry

    in me drown

Nietzsche

    In Donne

I envy being mercurial

    I can drink

first swallowed whole

    a dark musky vintage

then coughed up unscathed

    sensual and spiritual

uncorrupted opaque

    singing of experience

laved in mystery

    its lethal beauty

February Sky

"endlessly making an end to things"
—Celan

I must have left a fingerprint, a molecule of oil,

    a seal, a slick when I took my hands away

from her throat—the way she liked in loving

    to have her pearls exchanged for the torque

of my fingers and so kill her eminence for a second.

    The queen is dead. Long live the queen. The evidence

was volatile, was fugitive, was a story told

    in menstrual blood and glycerines, Chanel and boss

sauce. It failed in the telling to be events

    and sequence, the spell of water and bridge, and became

rain and distance, the first faint smell of rose

    dismembering, masking the rigor mortis of the coyotes.

I took my hands away as from the child

      sleeping or from the hot stove, and I was no longer I.

I saw the sky in the windshield of another city.

      The sky an empty karate studio, the sky Route 95.

Because she saw herself everywhere,

      The sky a fugue, the folds of a gown where the dragons are.

there could be no other. A film was her darling,

      the sky Artists' Supplies, the sky six-thirty darkening.

a mirror of her hair—fixed or deranged

      Sky of correspondences, the color of G minor, the taste of gray.

She thought, from the audience: *I should be up there*.

      February sky a copy center, relocated elsewhere.

I loved to go out into the audience, the bebopist said,

      and walk in the crowd to feel

what they feel. Jumping down from the bandstand, I

      broke my foot, lay there, had to blare it from my back.

The sky nineteenth-century smoke, the sky a drum,

then here comes the bass solo.

Vote Hoffa, the sky says, labor sky, the dollar soaring with the yen.

The sky popularized, blue-red, the access and the factory.

I take myself to the movies—the romance of sheets,

the dustup of things and her magnificent face: stylish,

the sky inside her eyes, chlorine and glass.

I tithe to the darkness and I'm glad for the dark

two hours where I undo her, where I remember the eye

I indulged, the opposite of sacrifice, the lamb's throat

uncut, the woolly body kindled in the green

like a dream of Lorca's, betrayed in the telling.

The sky Repairables, the sky Pony Rides.

Some nights in the house by the river, I walked out

into a collective dream of home—an overstory

overlooking a body of water—where I found

the horse like smoke or luck, a muscled earth, an avatar,

and I held him, face to flank, and felt the skeleton

under the skin and the fear of the human touched back

      by hunger. The great white eye another moon.

It was a lesser and a greater form of the feeling

      after fucking, if it has a form, if its past is present.

Sky an empty shelf in the Salvation Army Thrift Store.

      A few fine hairs like her lashes on my hands

The sky a white peony, the sky a paper life.

      when I came back and found her bound in the sheets,

the opposite of spectacle, not absorbing the gaze but

      giving off light like night water, giving back the gorgeous

I had inscribed there, a fallen form, small, fursheen, film

      still, a body suddenly small enough to fill a tear duct.

The sky a shell, a lull in the shelling.

      What was it like, the loving? Like Sarajevo

under siege, no electricity, no gas, no water,

      and yet the dance goes on in which a bathtub is filled,

and, although the theater is twenty degrees, the dancer

of the god-kissed tendons for her finale

jumps into it—the leap that takes away the breath

and rations it to everyone, and

it's the only bath for anyone in two months.

The sky orchestra and karma, the sky Gold Bought and Sold.

The windows of the house I won't live in held light

and the island fires on the river, held hawk and heron.

Under siege in dream, the panes slash my face when they shatter

with difference, inside, outside, with distance, what was

not. A second dream: kids go by on bikes and big wheels,

their faces grown up and disfigured, scabbed,

hydrocephalic with sadness. Finally the whole body

The sky a gray whale, the sky magnanimous and cruel.

and not just its parts, wants to be unloved, beginning

The sky Purgatory Road, the sky a god mouth, a crow.

with its parts, the fetish of her: a cell from the lining,

       spit, a follicle, the thousand ships of her face,

the torso and ratio, rib whittle, unbound feet, beginning

       to become vast, nothing you can touch, a taste,

The sky a copper pot blackened, picked clean of *puchero*.

       a smell, familiar and far away, unlocked by thaw,

feral and essential, like a language lost, like night

       illuminated by the night.

To Persephone Whose Face Is Potent
Against the Malice of Ghosts

after Sappho

Leave Philadelphia and come to the renovated
downtown where the starlings sweep through
at dusk and chatter in the ledges of the Savings
and Loan that a decade made delicious
       thresholds for the body.

Here where No More Kings plays Lupo's
Heartbreak Hotel from the stolen songbook
of Memphis, Macon, and Muscle Shoals
and divides the night into the desire to be held
       and the rain in A-flat.

Here the stone roses on the cornices cast down
their fragrance on the commerce of man boy,
boy girl, girl girl love and the frankincense
of fried dough flavors our others with hunger
       even into our dream.

In the plaza where the men in the nitrogen
cycle and the women nourished by bouquets
of nicotine want bus fare and spring
to sleep unwrapped and wake to the resins
       of the river.

Here, Persephone, look in all three
dimensions at once with your great
radiant face that we may be protected
from the shades in the gardens
            of our want and shame and love.